HOW TO KEEP WARM in WINTER

By DAVE ROSS

Thomas Y. Crowell
New York

Dedicated to
my blanket and warm fuzzy slippers

Library of Congress Cataloging in Publication Data
Ross, David, 1949–
How to keep warm in winter.

SUMMARY: Presents humorous advice for clothing,
activities, and devices for keeping warm in winter.
1. Dwellings—Heating and ventilation—Juvenile
literature. 2. Energy conservation—Juvenile
literature. 3. Clothing, Cold weather—Juvenile
literature. 4. Winter—Juvenile literature.
[1. Winter—Anecdotes, facetiae, satire, etc.]
I. Title.
TH7224.R66   741.5'973   79-6838
ISBN: 0-690-04060-1 (PAPER)
ISBN: 0-690-04077-6 (LB)

CONTENTS

Cold Facts

The world's largest snowflake landed in Cooke City, Montana, on April 2, 1949. It reportedly weighed 217 pounds.

The coldest-ever cold shoulder was recorded on January 14, 1979. Given by Ms. Mary Garrison of Cincinnati, Ohio, to her boyfriend, it registered 22° F.

The quickest winter on record hit what is now Goosebump, Idaho, 27,000 years ago. A giant glacier swept through the area at 50 miles per hour, instantly freezing everything in its path.

Warmed-over Facts

The warmest human temperature ever—116° F.—was reached in Schenectady, New York, on June 12, 1965, by Mr. James Gapczynski while he lay stricken from the bite of a South American Killer Lightning Bug.

The worst heat wave ever measured was over 33 feet tall. It struck Sweatsock, Nevada, on August 6, 1971, and melted everything in sight.

The world's record for reheated leftovers belongs to Mrs. Ruby Lovelace, who served her husband the same plate of beans 26 times.

WARM-UPS #1, #2 & #3

Paint your walls red and paste pictures of warm places on your windows.

Replace all the light bulbs in your house with sunlamps.

Listen to the Miami weather report.

Be friendly to people who hug a lot.

WARM-UPS #5 & #6

Think embarrassing thoughts
to make yourself blush.

Fill your swimming pool with hot chocolate
and pretend you're a marshmallow.

WARM-UPS #7, #8 & #9

Carry the torch in
the next Winter Olympics.

Sit in a bun warmer.

Wash your underwear
in hot-pepper sauce.

HOT TIPS #1 & #2

Get a job as a fire-eater.

Fireproof your pockets and carry hot charcoal.
(A good protection against pickpockets.)

HOT TIPS #3 & #4

Hang out with hotheads.

Visit insulting people so you can
become hot under the collar.

HOT TIP #5

Sell your soul.

HOT TIPS #8, #9 & #10

Juggle hot potatoes.

Grow hot peppers.

Buy a hot car.

COOL MANEUVER #1

Be kind to your furnace.

COOL MANEUVERS #2 & #3

Buy a very large chicken
and wear an egg costume.

Hijack a fuel-oil truck.

COOL MANEUVER #4

Spend the winter on the moon.
(Stay on the sunny side.)

ENERGY CONSERVATION IDEA #1

Drill an oil well in your backyard.
(Even if you don't strike oil, the
exercise will warm you up.)

ENERGY CONSERVATION IDEAS #2 & #3

Dress like a bear and go hibernate.

Store summer sunshine
in jars.

ENERGY CONSERVATION IDEA #4

Install your furniture on the ceiling.
(Warm air rises.)

ENERGY CONSERVATION IDEAS #5 & #6

Run a fever.

Get a job with the government and
bring home red tape to burn.

ENERGY CONSERVATION IDEA #7

Capture a fire-breathing dragon.

TOASTY WINTER FASHION HINTS #1 & #2

Wear long underwear.
(Be sure to get the right size.)

Have a suit made out of electric eels.

TOASTY WINTER FASHION HINTS #3, #4 & #5

Put a mitten
on your nose.

Wear six pairs
of socks.

Make a snowsuit out of an electric blanket
and buy a very long extension cord.

TOASTY WINTER FASHION HINT #6

Train fuzzy caterpillars
to sit on your ears.

COLD-WEATHER INVENTIONS #1 & #2

Install a giant magnifying glass over your house.
(Be careful not to focus.)

Turn your freezer dial to REVERSE
and make heat cubes.

COLD-WEATHER INVENTION #3

Fill a diving suit with hot chicken soup.
(Noodles are optional.)

COLD-WEATHER INVENTIONS #4, #5 & #6

For the cold classroom...

Solar desk warmer

(Be sure to get a seat near the window.)

Electric pencil
(Helps keep fingers warm.)

Hot-water-bottle book

FREEZE-PROOF SLEEPING AIDS #1 & #2

Have a hot spring installed in your bed.

Sleep with three dogs.

FREEZE-PROOF SLEEPING AID #3

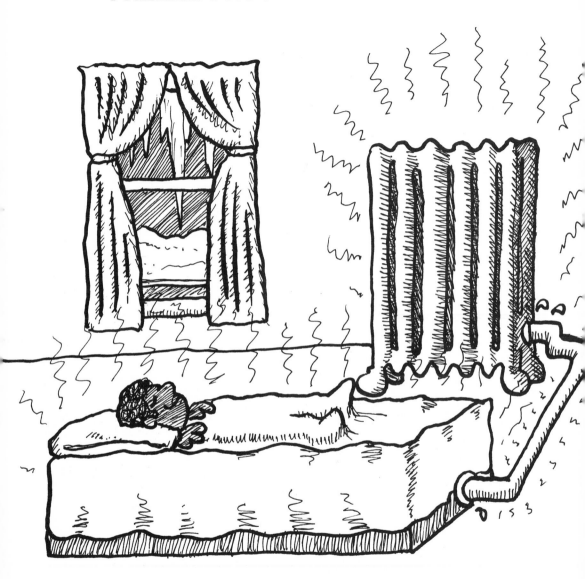

Connect your water bed to a radiator.

FREEZE-PROOF SLEEPING AID #4

Combine a sleeping bag with a toaster so you can be warm and still get up on time. (Be careful not to change the setting.)

WHEN ALL ELSE FAILS...

Deep-freeze yourself for the winter and
arrange to be thawed out in the spring.